DRUGS the facts about
ECSTASY

DRUGS **the facts about**

ECSTASY

SUZANNE LEVERT

BENCHMARK BOOKS

MARSHALL CAVENDISH
NEW YORK

Series Consultant: Dr. Amy Kohn, Chief Executive Officer, YWCA
of White Plains and Central Westchester, New York.
Thanks to John M. Roll, PhD, Director of Behavioral
Pharmacology at UCLA Integrated Substance Abuse Programs,
for his expert reading of this manuscript.

Benchmark Books
Marshall Cavendish
99 White Plains Road
Tarrytown, NY 10591-9001
www.marshallcavendish.us

Library of Congress Cataloging-in-Publication Data

LeVert, Suzanne.
The facts about ecstasy / Suzanne LeVert.
p. cm. — (Drugs)
Includes bibliographical references and index.
ISBN 0-7614-1807-5
1. Ecstasy (Drug)—Juvenile literature. I. Title. II. Series: Drugs (Benchmark Books)

RM666.M35L48 2005
362.29'9—dc22
2004009341

Photo research by Joan Meisel

Cover photo: Andrew Brooks/Corbis
Corbis: Andrew Brooks, 1, 2–3, 4–5; Scott Houston, 6, 17, 20; The Cover Story, 14; Bettmann, 61;
Tom Stewart, 72. Getty Images: Joe Raedle/Newsmakers, 10; AFP, 33;
Alex Wong, 49; Mark Wilson, 52; OFF/AFP, 64; Nucleus Medical Art: 41.
Photo Researchers, Inc.: Joubert, 22; Mike Agliolo, 25; John Bavosi. 26.

Printed in China

3 5 6 4 2

CONTENTS

A RAVE GIRL DANCES AT STARSCAPE 2000 IN BALTIMORE, MARYLAND. RAVES EMERGED IN THE UNITED KINGDOM IN THE MID-1980S AND GAINED AN UNDERGROUND FOLLOWING THROUGHOUT EUROPE AND THEN THE UNITED STATES.

1 ECSTASY: THE NUMBER ONE CLUB DRUG

ADAM. EVE. LOVE. X. A drug with a very long chemical name (methylenedioxymethamphetamine), abbreviated MDMA, has many different nicknames, but it is most commonly known as Ecstasy. Use of MDMA among teenagers and young adults today is widespread.

Euphoric. Loving. Open. Users of MDMA often describe their first experiences with MDMA as involving feelings of empathy and compassion for others, along with a sense of relaxation and self-confidence. Those effects make the drug particularly attractive to teenagers, who typically struggle with issues of self-esteem and self-confidence as they grow into adults.

Too hot. Sweating uncontrollably. Racing heartbeat. Can't stop clenching my jaw. Although feelings of euphoria are the best-known reactions to taking MDMA, there are a number of very negative and dangerous side effects, such as a rise in body temperature and heart rate.

Depressed. Angry. Lonely. Exhausted. When the immediate effects of this drug wear off, which they tend to do about four to six hours after intake, most people explain that they feel slightly ill, very tired, and often depressed. These effects of withdrawing from the drug make it clear that MDMA is indeed a powerful substance that causes many changes in the brain and body, a number of them dangerous and some of them life-threatening.

Promiscuous. Dishonest. Ashamed. Some users feel anxious and depressed after using MDMA, probably not because of any effect of the drug itself, but rather because of their own behavior while under its influence. MDMA is an illegal drug, which means that those who buy it and use it must hide this fact from others, including parents, siblings, friends who don't use the drug, and teachers. Furthermore, the feelings of openness and empathy triggered by MDMA may lead to sexual behavior that many people regret after they come down from the high.

Desperate. Yearning. Anxious. Uncomfortable in my own skin. The more regularly people take MDMA, the more likely they are to become psychologically, if not physically, addicted. Scientists have been studying the short- and long-term effects of MDMA on the human brain and body for decades. Recent animal and human studies indicate that MDMA may cause permanent damage to certain brain cells, resulting memory loss, depression, and other medical problems.

Statistics show that nearly 9 percent of high school students in the United States have tried Ecstasy at one time or another—and estimates of use among college students are even higher. Further evidence indicates that Ecstasy use may be falling. Dr. Alan I. Leshner, director of the National Institute on Drug Abuse, reported in a 2001 interview, "It's the stealth drug amidst all the falling drug use. . . . Parents should be concerned."

Indeed, both parents and teenagers should be concerned because using Ecstasy contributed to more than 160 deaths between 1974 and 2000 and has put the health of thousands more at grave risk. The Drug Abuse Warning Network reported that emergency room admissions involving MDMA increased from 4,511 in 2000 and peaked in 2001 with 5,542. Since then, MDMA-related emergency room visits have declined, as has reported

TECHNO OR HOUSE MUSIC, STROBE LIGHTS, AND LASERS ARE TYPICAL OF RAVES AND DANCE CLUBS. WHILE SOME YOUNG PEOPLE USE DRUGS LIKE ECSTASY TO ENHANCE THE EXPERIENCE, MANY ATTEND THESE PARTIES SOBER, ENJOYING THE MUSIC AND THE ATMOSPHERE.

Ecstasy use among teens. According to the Drug Enforcement Administration (DEA), for instance, less than four thousand admissions to emergency rooms were linked to Ecstasy use in 2002.

Effects and Side Effects: Not So Ecstatic

What exactly is Ecstasy and what makes it so popular? The chemicals that make up MDMA act in unique ways in the brains and bodies of those who take the drug. A hit of Ecstasy triggers reactions in the body similar to those of two other types of drugs: amphetamines, or speed, and hallucinogens, such as LSD. Someone who takes Ecstasy is likely to experience an increase in blood pressure and heart rate, as well as an increase in overall physical energy. At the same time, users report feelings similar to those caused by hallucinogenic drugs. Although most users do not hallucinate, they do feel as if all of their senses—sight, sound, smell, taste, and in particular touch—are especially acute. Users may experience overwhelming feelings of empathy for others and a deep sensation of well-being and relaxation. These effects have become the hallmarks of the Ecstasy experience.

This combination of an increase in energy and a sense of euphoria has made MDMA popular with teenagers, who want to dance and party together but typically feel insecure and uncomfortable in social situations. That is why the use of Ecstasy remains most common in dance clubs, especially at all-night or even all-weekend parties called raves. It may also explain the persistent myth that MDMA is safe and offers nothing more than a pleasant high. However, research continues to indicate that even casual users put their health and their lives at risk every time they take the drug.

Another reason for MDMA's popularity is its price. For about the cost of a movie and pizza (about twenty dollars), a teenager can purchase a tablet of Ecstasy. This dose, called a hit, will trigger a high that will last anywhere from two to five hours. Many users will "bump" the drug, taking a second dose when the initial dose begins to fade. Obviously, bumping doubles the financial cost of taking the drug. It also places more stress on the brain and body, making it even more toxic.

MDMA triggers changes in two primary systems of the body: the cardiovascular system (the heart and blood vessels) and the central nervous system (the brain and brain chemicals). These changes cause both physical and psychological symptoms.

Physically MDMA causes the heart to beat faster and less efficiently and raises blood pressure as well. It also disrupts the body's ability to regulate its internal temperature, which leads to serious, even deadly, dehydration (lack of sufficient fluid). These effects can lead to dangerous increases in body core temperature. MDMA also decreases appetite and suppresses the need for sleep, making exhaustion a distinct and frequent side effect.

Because MDMA acts on brain cells, it should come as no surprise that using the drug results in many psychological symptoms and side effects. The brain sends messages to cells throughout the brain and body by the use of natural chemicals called neurotransmitters. MDMA disturbs the delicate balance of these chemicals, specifically causing a marked rise in a chemical called serotonin. Serotonin is necessary for a wide variety of bodily functions, including the regulation of sleep, memory, and mood. As a result, those who use MDMA often suffer from a range of problems, including sleep disorders, memory loss, depression, and anxiety.

Whether or not the psychological and physical effects and side effects of using MDMA are permanent is still under investigation. The most recent animal and human studies indicate that MDMA may indeed cause lasting damage, especially to the still-developing brains of teenagers who take it.

Unfortunately, scientists have difficulty tracking the effects of MDMA. Most young people who take Ecstasy take it while consuming other illicit substances, particularly marijuana, amphetamines, and other so-called club drugs such as ketamine and fentanyl, two powerful tranquilizers. Drinking alcohol while taking MDMA is also common. It is therefore difficult to discern which side effects are caused by

SOME VENUES HAVE ECSTASY-TESTING STANDS WHERE PILLS ARE TESTED FOR PURITY.

MDMA, which are caused by other substances, and which result from ingesting those substances in combination.

Something else complicating scientists' research is the possibility that the pills sold in dance clubs and on college campuses are not pure MDMA. In one study, published in a 2000 *Journal of the American Medical Association,* scientists analyzed 107 pills received anonymously by the organization DanceSafe, which offers an Ecstasy tablet analysis service. The analysis showed that 63 percent contained some MDMA (but not pure MDMA), while 29 percent contained other identifiable drugs but no MDMA. The most common drug identified other than MDMA was dextromethorphan, which is the active ingredient in over-the-counter cough syrups. The doses of dextromethorphan in the Ecstasy pills ranged from 4.5 to 9 times higher than the usual therapeutic doses. Such an overdose of an otherwise helpful medication can lead to detrimental side effects, such as irregular heartbeat, psychosis, and mood swings.

The Origins of Ecstasy

Ecstasy often is dubbed a designer drug because it is created in laboratories out of man-made chemicals to produce specific effects. This property makes it different from other illegal drugs that come from natural sources, such as cocaine (from the coca leaf), marijuana (from the hemp plant), and heroin (from the poppy). Cocaine, marijuana, and heroin, among other "natural" drugs, have been illegal for many decades.

When people first started using Ecstasy and other designer drugs—including ketamine, fentanyl, MPPP, and GHB—for recreational purposes, they avoided the laws already enacted against the sale and use of the so-called natural drugs. But today MDMA is just as illegal as heroin, marijuana, and cocaine and those who possess it, use it, or sell it are subject to criminal prosecution and imprisonment. About 80 percent of Ecstasy is produced in western Europe, primarily in the Netherlands. The chemicals necessary to manufacture MDMA, as well as the drug itself, are banned in the United States.

A Brief History of Ecstasy

The German drug company Merck first created MDMA in 1914. Produced during the manufacture of another drug, MDMA was not used in a clinical setting or tested on humans until the 1970s. In 1978 two psychiatrists, Alexander (Sasha) Shulgin and Dave Nichols, synthesized quantities of MDMA and used it in their therapy sessions with patients. Shulgin and Nichols published a scientific article about the drug's effect on humans, noting that people who took it were able to be more open and empathetic, paving the way, they said, to more productive therapy sessions.

DR. ALEXANDER SHULGIN, MDMA RESEARCHER, IN HIS LAB.

During the 1990s, Ecstasy became popular at clubs and other venues where dance parties called raves took place. At a rave, a group of young people crowds into a large venue—an empty warehouse, an open field, a dance club—and, with techno music blaring and lights flashing, dances the night (and maybe even the entire weekend) away. Taking Ecstasy, users believe, heightens the experience of these dance parties, and Ecstasy's popularity grew as the rave culture spread throughout the United States. But ravers are not the only people who take Ecstasy. Use has spread from rave parties to high schools and college campuses and even to middle schools.

PERCENT OF STUDENTS REPORTED USING MDMA AT LEAST ONCE DURING THEIR LIFETIMES

YEAR	1999	2000	2001	2002	'01-'02 CHANGE
8TH GRADE	2.7	4.3	5.2	4.3	-.09
10TH GRADE	6.0	7.3	8.0	6.6	-1.4
12TH GRADE	8.0	11.0	11.7	10.5	-1.2

Source: The Monitoring the Future Study 2003

Ecstasy Today

Without question, Ecstasy use is fairly common, especially among teenagers. In 2000, 8 percent of U.S. high school seniors surveyed said they had tried it at least once. Results from the 2001 Monitoring the Future survey, conducted by the National Institute on Drug Abuse, indicated that MDMA use increased among students in twelfth, tenth, and eighth grade in 2000. For twelfth and tenth graders, 2000 was the second consecutive year that MDMA use increased. Among twelfth graders, lifetime use increased from 8 to 11 percent, which means that one in nine seniors had tried Ecstasy in his or her lifetime. However, since 2001, reported use of Ecstasy appears to be declining. According to the 2003 Monitoring the Future Study, 3.2 percent of eighth graders, 5.4 percent of tenth graders, and 8.3 percent of twelfth graders reported using MDMA at least once during their lifetimes.

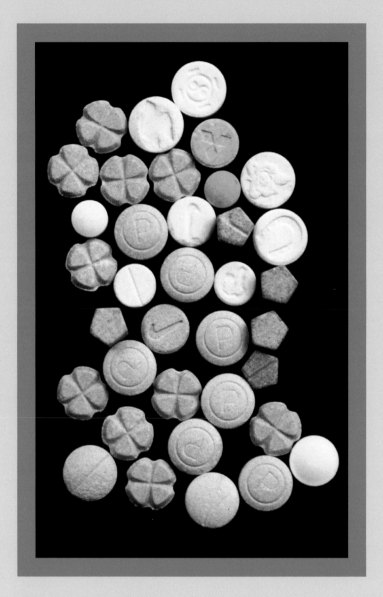

ECSTASY TABLETS HAVE DIFFERENT COLORS, SHAPES, AND STAMPS.

2 DRUGS BY DESIGN

MEN AND WOMEN have used substances to alter their perceptions and feelings—both for religious and spiritual reasons, and as a rather dangerous form of recreation and experimentation—for thousands of years. From alcohol to nicotine to marijuana and heroin, and now to designer drugs such as MDMA, natural and man-made substances that change one's feelings and the way one perceives the world have been a part of society throughout history.

MDMA is a combination of drugs that are chemically similar to the stimulant methamphetamine and the hallucinogen mescaline. This combination of substances triggers many changes in the human body, including altering the balance of chemicals in the

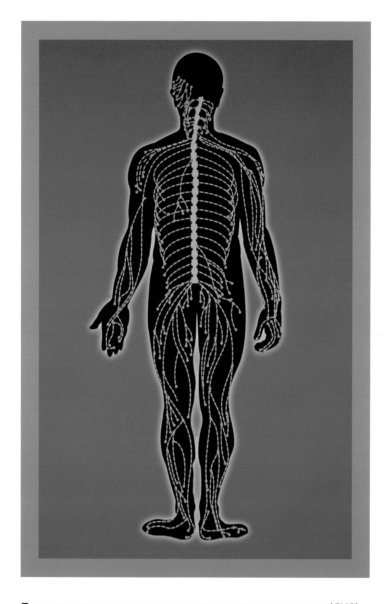

THE BRAIN AND SPINAL CORD MAKE UP THE CENTRAL NERVOUS SYSTEM (CNS).
THE THIRTY-ONE PAIRS OF NERVES THAT BRANCH OFF THE SPINAL CORD CARRY
NERVE IMPULSES FROM THE CNS TO VARIOUS STRUCTURES OF THE BODY (SKIN,
SKELETAL MUSCLE, INTERNAL ORGANS, GLANDS) AND BACK. NERVES OUTSIDE OF
THE CNS ARE PART OF THE PERIPHERAL NERVOUS SYSTEM.

brain. Some of these chemical changes can cause very pleasant short-term feelings of euphoria and empathy, which make the drug popular with young people and may prove to make it a useful medication in the treatment of certain mental illnesses. However, recent evidence shows that some of these changes in brain chemistry may cause long-term damage.

Understanding the Brain

The human brain and nervous system form a vast communications network. Every emotion felt, action taken, and physiological function undergone is processed through the brain to the nerve fibers, which extend down the spinal cord and throughout the body.

The brain itself is divided into several regions, each responsible for performing certain activities. The brain stem, located at the base of the skull, controls such basic physiological functions as heart rate and respiration. The cerebral cortex is the largest and most highly developed portion of the brain, where the activities we define as "thinking"— thought, perception, memory, and communication—take place.

On top of the brain stem and buried under the cortex is the limbic system. Scientists believe this highly complex, and still largely unmapped, region is home base to our emotions. It receives and regulates emotional information and helps govern appetite, stress, and desire.

Perhaps the most treasured human quality is human emotion, with all its extraordinary variety and depth—sadness, joy, dread, regret, anticipation, awe. This variety is a sign of health and vitality. While everyone has a unique personality and range of moods, good mental health requires balance— the ability to experience joy as well as sadness, anger as well as passivity, contentedness as well as frustration.

For this to occur, brain cells must be able to communicate with one another, to send messages from one cell to another, from one center of brain activity to the next. Drugs like MDMA interfere with this communications network.

Getting the Message Across: The Synapse

How does the information one takes in, through reading for example, pass through the parts of the brain that recognize letters and comprehend words and then go on to the limbic system to trigger emotions such as excitement and joy? To answer these questions, scientists study not only the anatomy of the brain—its large structures and organization—but also the biochemical processes that take place among the tiniest cells of the nervous system, called neurons.

Each neuron contains three important parts: the central body, the dendrites, and the axon. Messages from other neurons enter the cell body through the dendrites, which are branchlike projections that extend from the cell body. Once the central body processes the messages, it can pass on the information to its neighboring neuron through a cablelike fiber, called the axon. At incredible speeds, information covering every aspect of human physiology, emotion, and thought zips through the body from one neuron to another in this way.

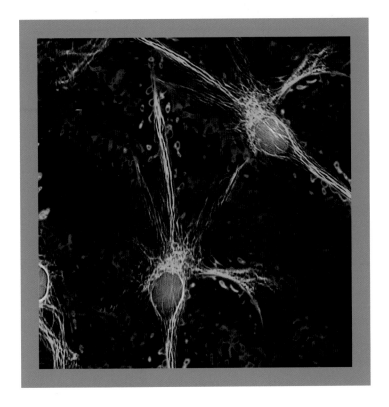

NERVE CELLS, OR NEURONS, ARE IN THE BRAIN AND SPINAL CORD AND THROUGHOUT THE BODY. EACH NEURON HAS A LARGE CELL BODY WITH SEVERAL LONG PROCESSES—AXONS AND DENDRITES—EXTENDING FROM IT.

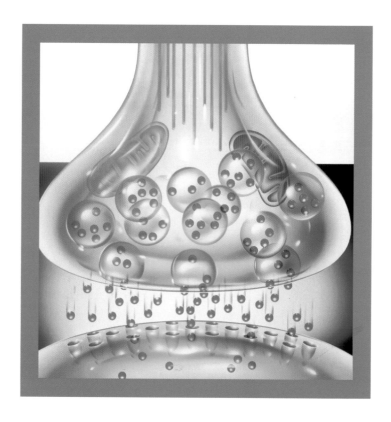

THIS ILLUSTRATION SHOWS A NERVE IMPULSE PASSING ACROSS THE SYNAPSE BETWEEN TWO NERVE CELLS. NEUROTRANSMITTERS ARE SHOWN IN RED.

But the axon of one neuron does not attach directly to its neighboring neuron. Instead, a tiny gap—called a synapse—separates them. For a message to cross a synapse, it requires the help of natural chemicals called neurotransmitters, which are stored in packets at the end of each nerve cell.

When a cell is ready to send a message, its axon releases a certain amount and type of neurotransmitter. This chemical then travels across the synapse to bind to special molecules called receptors, which sit on the surfaces of all cells in the body and bind to specific chemicals. Receptors are very complex structures. They have sites into which very specific neurotransmitter molecules fit, much like a lock-and-key mechanism. The neurotransmitter molecules from the first neuron are the keys and the receptors on the second neuron are the locks. When the key enters the lock by binding to the receptor molecule, the lock operates and the transmission of the message is complete.

In neurons, the receptors sit on the dendrites of the adjacent nerve cell. To send a message, the first cell releases the appropriate neurotransmitter into the synapse. When that neurotransmitter fits into the right receptor on the second cell, the second cell receives the message. Once that occurs, any neurotransmitter left in the synapse gets sucked back into the neuron that released it, in a process called reuptake.

Neurotransmitters: Body and Mind

The ways in which illicit drugs such as MDMA can alter how mood and perception occur in the brain are linked to three neurotransmitters. One of these, Serotonin, influences a wide range of brain activities, including appetite, hormone secretion, and heart rate. If a person does not produce enough serotonin anxiety, the mood disorder called depression, and other psychological problems often result. MDMA acts directly on the ways the brain produces and uses serotonin.

MDMA also affects brain levels of dopamine, another crucial neurotransmitter. Dopamine follows two main pathways in the brain. One pathway connects to a portion of the brain that controls movement. When this pathway malfunctions because of an imbalance of dopamine, then problems with movement occur, as is the case with Parkinson's disease. The other dopamine pathway extends into the limbic system. When dopamine does not exist in proper amounts or is unable to reach the organs of the limbic system, emotional problems such as depression and mood swings may develop.

Norepinephrine is the third neurotransmitter affected by MDMA and other illicit drugs. Norepinephrine is an especially important chemical during times of physical or emotional stress. It acts to stimulate the nervous system to raise blood pressure, increase heart rate, and open up air

"Everyone told me that taking X was like having a beer," admits Patrick, now a sixteen-year-old junior in high school.

It'd make you feel great for a few hours and then you'd be fine. No hangover, no fuss, no muss. A trip on X is called rolling, and that's what it felt like: Rolling on a good time. The first couple of times I took it, it was fantastic. I didn't take much of it—just a couple of tabs on a couple of nights— and I felt great. I loved everybody around me and felt like they loved me. I used to be so edgy around other people—I never could relax—so it was great. But the next time I did it, I did a lot of it over a long weekend. I don't think I slept for thirty-six hours. I was sweating so much, drinking so much water. I ended up just exhausted. Then, when I crashed, I woke up feeling lousy. Depressed. Anxious. And I'd forget stuff, like which books to take to school. I was back to normal within a few weeks, but it was an odd feeling. It scared me. I won't take it again.

passages to the lungs. These actions provide more oxygen to the muscles, preparing them to mobilize if necessary—a response that is often called flight-or-fight syndrome.

All three of these neurotransmitters must be present in the right amounts, and in the right balance, for the human brain to work properly. Any number of circumstances and substances can create an imbalance, including the use and abuse of substances like MDMA.

Ecstasy: The Chemistry

The drug MDMA has two so-called parents—hallucinogens and amphetamines, including methamphetamine. Indeed, MDMA has several properties, including its chemical structure, that are similar to each of these types of drugs.

Speed Kills

Amphetamines first became available over-the-counter as a treatment for colds and flu. In addition to clearing stuffy noses, however, users of these early amphetamines also experienced increased energy, decreased appetites, and elevated moods. Today, smaller amounts of these substances are still used in cold formulas, and some overweight people take prescription amphetamines as a weight-loss aid.

Amphetamines work by increasing the amount of the three neurotransmitters serotonin, norepinephrine, and dopamine. They do so by attaching to the receptors for those chemicals on the surfaces of neurons and pushing the neurotransmitters out into the synapses between brain cells. The extra neurotransmitters cause a host of physical and psychological changes. Users experience feelings of euphoria and self-confidence, increased attention and alertness, and a decrease in appetite. However, the same drugs often cause paranoia, aggression, and anxiety. Physically, amphetamines act to increase blood pressure and heart rate, increase blood sugar, and raise body temperature. When they are taken in large doses, these physical reactions to the drugs can be fatal, most commonly by causing heart attacks and strokes.

Altering Reality

Hallucinogens represent the other parent of MDMA. Hallucinogens are drugs that change how the brain processes thoughts, moods, and perceptions. The most commonly used and abused hallucinogen is LSD, which binds to and activates a specific receptor for the neurotransmitter serotonin. Normally, serotonin binds to and activates its receptors and then is taken back up into the neuron that released it. Just as MDMA and amphetamines do, LSD binds very tightly to the serotonin receptor, causing a greater than normal activation of the receptor and greater release of serotonin.

Because serotonin has a role in many of the brain's functions, activation of its receptors by LSD produces widespread effects, including rapid emotional swings, altered perceptions, and—if taken in large enough doses—delusions and visual hallucinations. Many people who take LSD report feeling anxious, paranoid, and nauseous, especially during the first hour or so after taking the drug. Aftereffects may include flashbacks, which are unexpected, disturbing recollections of visual events associated with the original drug experience.

Taking "X"

MDMA usually comes in pill form, synthesized out of raw ingredients in labs in Europe and the United States. MDMA pills come in several different colors, most commonly beige, yellow, and white. The strength of each dose of MDMA greatly varies from fifty milligrams to as much as three hundred milligrams. The effects of a dose of about one hundred milligrams reach their peak an hour or so after a person takes a tablet and last from about three to six hours. Frequent users of Ecstasy often experiment by taking three or more tablets at once, which they call stacking, or by consuming a series of pills over a short period of time, nicknamed piggybacking. The more MDMA someone takes, the greater the effects on the brain and body. These effects may result in immediate illness, permanent brain damage, and even death.

TIMOTHY LEARY, AN EARLY ADVOCATE OF LSD EXPERIMENTATION

Mixing But Not Matching:
X and Other Club Drugs

The risks of taking Ecstasy are not confined to the effects and side effects of MDMA itself, for two reasons. Most Ecstasy tablets purchased by young people at raves and at school are not made from pure MDMA. Instead, they contain other drugs, including some that are much more dangerous than MDMA, such as pure methamphetamine, ketamine, and even cocaine. And most Ecstasy users tend to use other drugs or alcohol at the same time, hoping to prolong or heighten the Ecstasy experience. Most often, marijuana is the second drug of choice, but some use cocaine, heroin, or another of the so-called club drugs. Among the most common club drugs are the following:

OTHER CLUB DRUGS

Official Name	Nickname
GHB (Gamma-hydroxybutyrate)	G, liquid Ecstasy
Rohypnol	Roofie, roche
Ketamine	Special K
LSD	Speed, ice, chalk, Meth
Fetanyl	Acid

Fentanyl. There are several analogues of the legal form of this drug, which doctors prescribe as a painkiller for medical patients undergoing surgery. It falls into the category of opioid drugs. Opioids are similar to opium, a painkiller derived from the poppy flower. A common, powerful opiate is morphine. Fentanyl and its analogues are about eighty times stronger than morphine. According to the National Institute on Drug Abuse, about 150 people die every year from fentanyl overdoses. Fentanyl kills by slowing down a user's breathing until it stops completely. The drug can also cause the chest muscles to contract so tightly that the lungs cannot expand to take in air. Those who overdose from it simply suffocate.

MPPP. MPPP is the most common analogue of the painkiller meperidine, also known as Demerol. Doctors often prescribe Demerol to patients to alleviate pain following surgery. It is highly addictive.

GHB (gamma hydroxybutyrate). Used as an anesthetic in Europe and once widely available in health food stores as a dietary supplement to build muscles, GHB now is a common drug of abuse among teens and young adults. GHB is a sedative that causes relaxation and mild euphoria when taken at low doses. At higher doses it can cause headaches, loss of consciousness, seizures, coma, and even death.

Rohypnol. Rohypnol is the trade name for a drug called flunitrazepam, also known as the date-rape drug because of the effect it has on people who take it together with alcohol. Rohypnol belongs to a class of drugs known as benzodiazepines, which are sedatives. Like other sedatives, including GHP and MPPP, Rohypnol causes people who take it at low doses to feel more relaxed and less anxious. With higher doses, people become light-headed and drowsy, and lack muscle coordination. It can also produce an effect called retrograde amnesia, which means that individuals may not remember events they experience while under the influence of the drug. When mixed with alcohol, Rohypnol can cause people to lose all muscle control, making them easy targets for sexual assault.

Ketamine and PCP. Ketamine is an anesthetic used primarily in veterinary medicine. Like its cousin PCP (phencyclidine), ketamine also produces hallucinations and delirium in those who take large doses. Both ketamine and PCP have so many different effects on brain activity because of their complicated chemistry. Taking PCP and Ketamine can produce a state similar to getting drunk, taking amphetamines, and taking a hallucinogen all at the same time. They also carry risks of side effects, including increased heart rate and death from seizures or heart attacks. Both of these drugs also can cause memory loss.

Without question, MDMA and related club drugs are powerful, even in their pure forms. Because they are produced at illegal underground labs, however, they produce not only dangerous effects and side effects but also unpredictable ones.

3 RISKY BUSINESS: THE BODY AND BRAIN ON X

IN THE UNITED STATES, the Food and Drug Administration (FDA) is responsible for protecting the public health by assuring the safety and effectiveness of human and veterinary drugs and other products. According to its own mission statement, "the FDA is also responsible for advancing the public health by helping to speed innovations that make medicines and foods more effective, safer, and more affordable; and helping the public get the accurate, science-based information they need to use medicines and foods to improve their health."

The FDA made it illegal for anyone to buy, sell, or possess MDMA—including physicians and their patients—once studies of the drug showed that it posed a risk to the public. The use of this illegal drug carries with it many risks to both mental health and physical well-being.

Effects and Side Effects of Ecstasy

MDMA's most common side effects are involuntary teeth clenching, a rise in body temperature that causes thirst and sweating, and dehydration. Users have developed several ways to cope with these effects. Some suck on pacifiers to alleviate teeth clenching; most drink a lot of water; and at many party sites there is a separate room that is dark, quiet, and cooler than the main party room.

These symptoms are typical for those who take a moderate amount of Ecstasy. Someone who takes an overdose of MDMA, which is easy to do because of the unregulated nature of Ecstasy production and sale, risks even more serious side effects. Symptoms of Ecstasy overdose include

- nausea
- difficulty talking
- vomiting
- inability to sweat
- racing heartbeat, even while at rest
- fainting
- tremors

- loss of muscle control
- problems urinating
- high blood pressure
- muscle cramping
- hyperthermia (high body temperature)
- kidney failure

In addition to the short-term effects of moderate use, recent research shows that MDMA may cause serious, and perhaps permanent, long-term damage to two systems of the body: the cardiovascular system and parts of the brain and central nervous system.

MDMA and the Cardiovascular System

Two of the neurotransmitters affected by MDMA are norepinephrine and serotonin. Both of these chemicals are involved in what scientists have termed the flight-or-fight stress response. Norepinephrine, serotonin, and other chemicals flow from neuron to neuron, triggering the heart to beat faster and the blood pressure to rise, preparing the body to either stay and fight or flee from danger. When someone takes MDMA, serotonin and norepinephrine are released, causing similar changes to the cardiovascular system.

Blood pressure. In a study presented to the National Institutes of Health in 2001, scientists measured blood pressure responses to MDMA in twelve

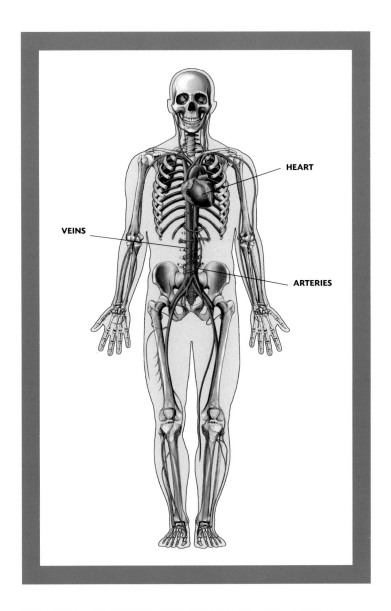

THE CARDIOVASCULAR SYSTEM CONSISTS OF THE HEART AND THE BLOOD VESSELS. ARTERIES (RED) CARRY BLOOD AWAY FROM THE HEART; VEINS (BLUE) RETURN BLOOD TO THE HEART. EVEN SMALL DOSES OF MDMA PRODUCE LARGE INCREASES IN BLOOD PRESSURE.

volunteers ranging in age from eighteen to forty with a history of MDMA use. They were startled to discover that even moderate doses of MDMA produced large increases in blood pressure—far greater than those seen when the same volunteers received doses of pure amphetamines. The rise in blood pressure was so great that the investigators chose not to test the subjects with the higher doses typically taken by users at raves.

Heart rate. During the same study scientists noted that the subjects' hearts beat faster and harder after they took MDMA. This rise in heart rate was also greater than the one measured after the subjects received pure amphetamines. Another study, reported in a 2000 issue of *Annals of Internal Medicine,* used echocardiography to view subjects' hearts while they were experiencing the effects of MDMA. Usually, when the heart beats faster, it also pumps blood more efficiently. But the hearts of the test subjects were not more efficient; they had to beat harder and use more oxygen than normal. This extra work may cause permanent heart damage, even a heart attack, in people with underlying heart problems who take the drug.

Research continues on the effects of MDMA on the cardiovascular system. So far, no studies exist that prove a connection between MDMA use and heart disease. However, the drug's effects on the cardiovascular system help explain some of the less serious, but often very uncomfortable, short-term side effects experienced by many users, including rapid heartbeat, breathlessness, and exhaustion.

MDMA and the Brain

MDMA acts directly on the brain to alter the way neurons release and use certain neurotransmitters, including serotonin, norepinephrine, and dopamine. This action disrupts the balance of these chemicals, which are responsible for a host of physiological and psychological functions. Among the effects and side effects related to this imbalance are the following:

Mood disorders. In a pilot study conducted in Ireland, one group of researchers enrolled sixteen light users (young people who had used MDMA fewer than twenty times) and twelve heavy users of MDMA (young people who had used MDMA more than twenty times). The researchers found that heavy MDMA users displayed a wide range of psychological problems, including obsessive behavior, anxiety, hostility, and paranoia.

Sleep disorders. In a study published in a 1993 *Sleep* magazine, researchers found that Ecstasy users experienced decreased total sleep time compared with nonusers. The same group of researchers studying a different group of users and nonusers reached a different result when they repeated the test: MDMA users spent more time in deep sleep than did nonusers. Even though the two studies gave conflicting results, it remains clear to researchers that the imbalances of neurotransmitters triggered by MDMA disrupt normal sleep patterns, causing users to sleep either more or less than usual.

Impulsiveness. When a person is impulsive, he or she acts without thinking, usually in order to increase his or her chances of having fun or feeling pleasure. In a study published in a 1998 *Neuropsychopharmocology,* investigators measured impulsiveness in three groups of volunteers: MDMA users who had also used other drugs, other drug users who had never used MDMA, and controls who had never used any illicit drug. Those in the MDMA group had more psychological problems and were more impulsive than those in the other two groups. In addition, the users who had consumed the most MDMA over the course of their lives received the highest impulsiveness scores.

Memory problems. Several studies have shown that MDMA users score much lower on tests that challenge their ability to recall facts than do nondrug users or users of drugs other than MDMA. In one study, reported in a 1999 issue of

Psychopharmacology and cited in the National Institute on Drug Abuse's extract *Ecstasy: What We Know and Don't Know,* volunteers were asked to listen to a sixty-five-word, audiotaped news story. Researchers then instructed them to write down all that they could remember, word for word, right away and then again forty minutes later. Members of the MDMA group scored substantially lower than either nondrug users or users of drugs other than MDMA.

Whether or not any of these physical and psychological changes to the brains of MDMA users are permanent remains the subject of a great deal of controversy. In an experiment that used red squirrel monkeys as subjects, researchers at The Johns Hopkins University demonstrated that just four days of exposure to the drug caused damage that persisted six to seven years later. Combining this result with the evidence about MDMA's effects on human users' memories, many scientists now believe that MDMA damages neurons that use the neurotransmitter serotonin to communicate with one another.

A brain-imaging study, also performed at The Johns Hopkins University, showed that people who had used MDMA had far fewer serotonin transporters—those sites on the ends of neurons that reuptake the unused serotonin left in the synapse—than did nonusers. This apparently permanent reduction of serotonin transporters occurred throughout the brain, and people who had used MDMA more often lost more of the transporters than those who had used less of the drug.

MDMA and Addiction

One of the most controversial questions about MDMA is whether or not it is addictive. As defined by Merriam-Webster's Collegiate Dictionary, addiction is a "compulsive need for and use of a habit- forming substance (as heroin, nicotine, or alcohol) characterized by tolerance and by well-defined physiological symptoms upon withdrawal; persistent compulsive use of a substance known by the user to be harmful."

Another definition comes from the *Diagnostics and Statistical Manual,* fourth edition (DSM-IV), a tome used by psychiatrists and other health professionals in diagnosing and treating mental illness. This manual defines substance dependence as a pattern of behavior occurring over a period of twelve or more months that includes at least three of the following:

• Substance is often taken in larger amounts or over longer period than intended. Persistent desire exists, or unsuccessful efforts are made, to cut down or control substance use.

• A great deal of time is spent in activities necessary to obtain the substance (e.g., visiting multiple doctors or driving long distances), use the substance, or recover from its effects. Important social, occupational, or recreational activities are given up or reduced because of substance use.

• The user continues substance use despite knowledge of having a persistent or recurrent psychological or physical problem that is caused or exacerbated by use of the substance.

In addition to exhibiting these behaviors, an addicted person will also develop tolerance to the drug, which the manual defines as either the need for markedly increased amounts of the substance in order to achieve intoxication or desired effect; or markedly diminished effect with continued use of the same amount.

Finally, symptoms of withdrawal from the drug may be present, which the manual defines as being either characteristic withdrawal syndrome for the substance (e.g., depression, anxiety, sleeplessness) or taking the same, or a closely-related, substance to relieve or avoid withdrawal symptoms.

Although MDMA does not appear to be addictive in the same way as heroin or cocaine for instance, several studies in both humans and animals suggest that MDMA users may risk becoming addicted to the substance. One study, published in a 2001 issue of *Human Psychopharmacology*, found that about 60 percent of fifty-two MDMA users reported symptoms of withdrawal, including feeling tired and weak, having a change in appetite, feeling depressed, and having trouble concentrating. Forty-three percent of those MDMA users met the DSM-IV criteria for dependence on MDMA.

MDMA: The Good News

In 2001 the FDA approved research into the use of MDMA as a medical treatment for a psychological condition called post-traumatic stress disorder (PTSD). PTSD is an anxiety disorder that can develop after someone experiences a terrifying event or ordeal. Traumatic events known to cause PTSD include violent personal assaults, such as rape or mugging; natural disasters, such as hurricanes or earthquakes; accidents; or military combat.

PTSD can be extremely disabling. Many people with PTSD repeatedly reexperience the ordeal in the form of flashback episodes, memories, nightmares, or frightening thoughts, especially when they are exposed to events or objects reminiscent of the trauma. Anniversaries of the event can

Vietnam veterans visit the Vietnam Veterans Memorial in Washington, D.C. About 30 percent of the men and women who served in the Vietnam War have experienced post-traumatic stress disorder.

also trigger symptoms. People with PTSD also experience emotional numbness and sleep disturbances, depression, anxiety, and irritability or outbursts of anger. Feelings of intense guilt are also common.

According to the National Institute of Mental Health, about 3.6 percent of U.S. adults ages eighteen to fifty-four (5.2 million people) experience PTSD during the course of a given year. About 30 percent of the men and women who served in the Vietnam War, about 1.7 million people, experience PTSD. PTSD has also been detected among veterans of the Persian Gulf War, with some estimates running as high as 8 percent.

Scientists researching MDMA as a treatment for PTSD hope that under careful medical supervision and using only the purest form of the drug, people with PTSD can explore their feelings about their trauma with more ease, openness, and trust—the very feelings a profound release of serotonin can engender.

If this research proves that MDMA can be used to help PTSD sufferers recover from this disabling disorder, then the FDA is likely to approve its use under strict medical supervision. This means that it would be illegal to use the drug without a doctor's prescription, and thus using it as a recreational drug at a rave or a club would remain illegal. The U.S. government takes drug laws very seriously, and the penalties for using MDMA illegally are strict and severe.

MARCH 31, 2004: RAF SOUCCAR (CENTER) OF THE ROYAL CANADIAN MOUNTED POLICE, U.S. DEPUTY ATTORNEY GENERAL JAMES COMEY, AND DEA ADMINISTRATOR KAREN TANDY ANNOUNCE ARRESTS IN CONNECTION WITH AN INTERNATIONAL INVESTIGATION TARGETING THE DRUG ECSTASY AND MARIJUANA-TRAFFICKING ORGANIZATIONS IN THE UNITED STATES AND CANADA.

4 ECSTASY AND THE LAW

USING MDMA IS a crime under both federal and state laws throughout the United States. Indeed, simply possessing one tablet of Ecstasy is a crime, even if the person holding it never intends to take it.

Using or possessing Ecstasy is a felony, which is a serious crime punishable by jail time or at least probation (court supervision) for up to five or sometimes ten years, depending on the state or federal law that applies. Usually the law sets the level of punishment based on the amount of the drug that one possesses. Manufacturing, distributing, and selling MDMA are also felonies. The penalty for these crimes can be even more severe than simply possessing or using the drug, and also depends on the amount of drug seized.

Drug Laws in the United States
Men and women have used so-called recreational drugs for centuries. Taking drugs to alter one's perceptions and mood, either for spiritual or social reasons, has long been a part of many world cultures. Native Americans smoked the leaves of the Cannibis sativa plant (more commonly known as marijuana) long before the Europeans arrived in the Americas. The religious rituals of the Native American Church still include the use of hallucinogens, and many who follow the Judeo-Christian tradition use alcohol as part of their rites.

As recently as the early twentieth century, drug use was legal—and common—in the United States. Alcohol was legal for more than three hundred years after the arrival of the *Mayflower,* then prohibited during the 1920s, only to be made legal again in the 1930s. Even marijuana was legal for more than a century until the U.S. government outlawed it in the 1930s. During the nineteenth century "patent medicines," so called because some producers obtained patents for the medications, were very common. Many of the patent medicines contained not only alcohol but also narcotics such as morphine, cocaine, and opium. Marketed as wonder cures for diseases ranging from the common cold to tuberculosis, these drugs were not only ineffective but also dangerous and sometimes addictive.

In the early twentieth century, U.S. legislators enacted laws that required manufacturers to list all the ingredients in these patent medicines as well as to support their claims for their effectiveness with scientific research. That legislation put an end to the patent medicine business and also set the stage for more stringent oversight by federal and state governments.

Today, drug laws in the United States are complicated. Each state has its own laws, which often differ from federal law. A branch of the U.S. Justice Department called the DEA is the primary drug enforcement agency in the United States. Its mission is to enforce the laws surrounding controlled substances and to penalize anyone found to be involved in growing, manufacturing, or distributing controlled substances in this country.

Scheduling Drugs by Law

In 1970 the U.S. Congress passed the Controlled Substances Act. Through this act, drugs are placed into one of five schedules, or categories. The FDA, with help from the DEA and medical experts, decides what schedule a drug belongs in based

Angela, a nineteen-year-old college freshman, was arrested for possession of five tablets of Ecstasy last year.

There's no other way to describe it: It was terrifying. The police arrested me when they stopped me for a speeding ticket. The little bag of pills fell right out of my purse when I reached for my wallet to show them my license. They arrested me on the spot.

Angela was taken to the police station and booked for possession of Ecstasy, which in her state (Louisiana) is a felony carrying a potential sentence of five years in jail.

I was terrified. I'm a premed student. If I had a felony arrest, I could be thrown out of school. Even if they didn't throw me out, it would be very difficult, if not impossible, to get into a medical school with a felony record. I couldn't believe my dream of becoming a doctor was going to end because of having a few pills of Ecstasy—which I wasn't even sure I wanted to take.

Luckily for Angela, the government offered her a program for first-time offenders with no previous record of arrests for violent crimes. Called Diversion, it requires at least six months of counseling and drug testing. If the offender meets all the requirements, the charges against him or her are dropped. "Believe me," Angela says, "I made every meeting, did everything I was told. Talk about 'scared straight.' I'll never forget it. Trust me, getting high for a few hours is not worth losing your freedom or your future."

upon several criteria: 1) the substance's medicinal value, 2) the substance's harmfulness, and 3) its potential for abuse or addiction. Schedule I is reserved for the most dangerous drugs that have no recognized medical use, while Schedule V is the classification used for the least dangerous drugs. The act also provides ways for new drugs to be added to or removed from a schedule based on new information about the drugs.

The factors that government officials use when deciding how to schedule a drug include:

1. Its actual or relative potential for abuse.
2. Scientific evidence of its pharmacological effect, if known.
3. The state of current scientific knowledge regarding the drug or other substance.
4. Its history and current pattern of abuse.
5. The scope, duration, and significance of abuse.
6. What, if any, risk there is to the public health.
7. Its psychological or physiological dependence liability.
8. Whether the substance is an immediate precursor (a chemical required for its manufacture) of a substance already controlled under the Controlled Substances Act.

DEA DRUG SCHEDULES

Schedule I

Examples:	Heroin, LSD, Marijuana, MDMA
Qualities:	(A) The drug or other substance has a high potential for abuse. (B) The drug or other substance has no currently accepted medical use in treatment in the United States. (C) There is a lack of accepted safety guidelines for use of the drug or other substance under medical supervision.

Schedule II

Examples:	Amphetamines, cocaine, fentanyl, Ritalyn
Qualities:	(A) The drug or other substance has a high potential for abuse. (B) The drug or other substance has a currently accepted medical use in treatment in the United States or a currently accepted medical use with severe restrictions. (C) Abuse of the drug or other substances may lead to severe psychological or physical dependence.

Schedule III

Examples:	Steroids, codeine
Qualities:	(A) The drug or other substance has a potential for abuse less than the drugs or other substances in Schedules I and II. (B) The drug or other substance has a currently accepted medical use in treatment in the United States. (C) Abuse of the drug or other substance may lead to moderate or low physical dependence or high psychological dependence.

Schedule IV

Examples:	Valium, Xanax, Rohypnol
Qualities:	(A) The drug or other substance has a low potential for abuse relative to the drugs or other substances in Schedule III. (B) The drug or other substance has a currently accepted medical use in treatment in the United States. (C) Abuse of the drug or other substance may lead to limited physical dependence or psychological dependence relative to the drugs or other substances in Schedule III.

Schedule V

Examples:	Cough syrups with codeine
Qualities:	(A) The drug or other substance has a low potential for abuse relative to the drugs or other substances in Schedule IV. (B) The drug or other substance has a currently accepted medical use in treatment in the United States. (C) Abuse of the drug or other substance may lead to limited physical dependence or psychological dependence relative to the drugs or other substances in Schedule IV.

Using these criteria, the FDA evaluates each new drug that comes into use—legally or illegally— and places it within one of five schedules. This helps state and federal lawmakers determine the penalty for possessing, manufacturing, or distributing the drug.

Ecstasy: Schedule I

In 1970 the FDA placed MDA on Schedule I. Illegal drug manufacturers quickly started producing the analogue MDMA, also known as Ecstasy, in an attempt to stay one step ahead of the law. In 1986 the U.S. Congress passed a law called the Controlled Substances Analogue Act. This act defines an analogue drug as any drug that has a chemical formula or effect on the body that closely resembles that of a drug already included in Schedules I or II. Most club drugs, including Ecstasy, are considered analogues and are thus subject to this act. Ecstasy is considered an analogue of two different types of scheduled drugs: methamphetamine and MDA, a synthetic hallucinogen used as an alternative to LSD.

Since 1988 Ecstasy has been a Schedule I drug, meaning that law enforcement officials consider it to have a great potential for abuse and addiction and that it poses a grave risk to public health. It also means that the DEA and other agencies

DRUG ENFORCEMENT ADMINISTRATION DEPUTY ASSISTANT ADMINISTRATOR GENE R. HAISLIP ANNOUNCES THE OUTLAWING OF ECSTASY IN MAY 1985. BOTH THE NONMEDICAL AND THE THERAPEUTIC USE OF MDMA WERE MADE ILLEGAL.

believe that scientists have performed enough research on the use and abuse of Ecstasy to place it in Schedule I. In the year 2000 Congress passed the Ecstasy Anti-Proliferation Act. This act directed the U.S. Sentencing Commission to provide increased penalties for the manufacture, importation, exportation, and trafficking of MDMA. Today, a first-time offender arrested with two hundred grams (about eight hundred tablets) of MDMA potentially faces a five-year sentence for his or her crime.

It should be noted that some scientists and physicians, and certainly many users of Ecstasy, have protested the inclusion of MDMA on Schedule I. It is true that MDMA appears to be far less physically addictive than heroin, marijuana, or cocaine. They also insist that the use of MDMA in a controlled psychiatric setting could be quite beneficial, as indicated by early reports of such use during the 1970s. However, because of the drug's placement on Schedule I, it has been difficult for scientists to test these benefits on humans. In the fall of 2001, however, the FDA gave the green light to the first such study, which would test Ecstasy's usefulness as a therapeutic tool to treat people with post-traumatic stress disorder. The results of that study will not be known for several years.

Even if there does prove to be some benefit to using MDMA under medical supervision, it does not change the fact that the drugs sold as Ecstasy on the underground market are hazardous, both to a person's health and to his or her freedom and future. Indeed, the road from the manufacture of the drug to an individual user's swallowing a pill is fraught with danger.

Traffic: The Underground World of Ecstasy Manufacture and Distribution

Most teenagers buy Ecstasy from a friend or acquaintance. It may seem to be a harmless and safe enough act, but the truth is that buying just one tablet of Ecstasy feeds into a vast criminal underground. It is a world that American law enforcement officials take very seriously.

Not an All-American Affair

MDMA is a man-made substance, made up of a variety of chemicals, all of which are banned in the United States and most European countries. The drug is generally made from chemicals called safrole, piperonal, and MDP2P. This combination produces a liquid product called Ecstasy oil, which is converted into powder by using solvents. The powder is then combined with a binding agent and formed into Ecstasy tablets.

FRENCH CUSTOMS OFFICERS SEIZED 100,000 ECSTASY TABLETS, SHOWN HERE, IN SEPTEMBER 2003, WHEN THEY STOPPED A SUSPICIOUS CAR COMING FROM BELGIUM INTO FRANCE.

Metal stamps are used to imprint designs on each tablet, often of cartoon characters or popular product logos.

Among the countries making the chemicals are Poland, Romania, Vietnam, and China, where government controls are more lax, and corrupt officials more available, than in the West. The controlled chemicals are commonly smuggled into the Netherlands—either by ship to Rotterdam, the busiest port in Europe and a forty-mile drive from southeastern Holland, or overland by truck, hidden in barrels among legitimate cargo. This takes advantage of virtually nonexistent frontier checks in the fifteen European Union countries, from Greece to the United Kingdom.

The Holland Connection

Laboratories located in the Netherlands produce about 80 percent of the Ecstasy found worldwide, though recent DEA statistics show an increasing number of labs located in the United States. Law enforcement seized seventeen clandestine Ecstasy laboratories in the United States in 2001 compared with seven seized in 2000. A typical lab produces 20 to 30 kilograms of Ecstasy per day. One kilogram yields approximately seven thousand tablets. At $20 to $30 per tablet, one kilogram of MDMA generates from $140,000 to $210,000 in income.

According to law enforcement experts, once the tablets are manufactured, European distributors smuggle the drug into the United States in shipments of about ten thousand or more tablets. They get the drugs into the United States in a number of different ways: through express mail services, with couriers aboard commercial airline flights, or in packages in air freight shipments from major European cities.

Once the drug is in the United States, evidence shows that largely foreign criminal organizations distribute it, including an Israeli crime syndicate and gangs made up of recent Russian immigrants to the United States. According to the U.S. Drug Enforcement Agency, other drug trafficking organizations based in the Dominican Republic, Asia, and Mexico have entered the Ecstasy trade. Furthermore, the DEA believes that cocaine from the Colombia drug cartel is being shipped to Europe in exchange for MDMA, which Colombian traffickers then distribute in the United States. Currently, the major gateway cities through which the drugs flow are Los Angeles, New York, and Miami. Once in the United States, traffickers manage to bring Ecstasy into nearly every community from coast to coast.

Why is the Netherlands the world's leading Ecstasy producer?

For a number of reasons connected to its history, domestic political considerations, and geography. For instance, smuggling has long thrived in the Netherlands's North Brabant region. For more than one hundred years, black marketers smuggled goods from adjacent Belgium in order to avoid Holland's high taxes. In the nineteenth century a bootleg liquor industry flourished deep in the forests of this region. Toward the end of World War II, black-market traders smuggled food and consumer goods from liberated areas of Belgium to the country's northern regions still occupied by the Nazis. Smuggling continued until 1999, when formation of a unified European Union eliminated most border controls and tariffs among member nations. Today, the two-lane roads running across the Belgian border have no check-points. Traffic passes unfettered in both directions.

Now, the North Brabant labs make Ecstasy. The distinctive odor of root beer or licorice the process gives off, which would be obvious in more densely populated areas, poses little problem among the woods and isolated farms. When a batch is finished, barrels are discarded in the countryside, and stolen vans used to transport them are burned to destroy evidence. Then, couriers laden with tiny tablets board airliners bound for the United States, or the traffickers use express mail or air freight packages to transport the goods.

Curbing the Tide of Ecstasy

The DEA persists in its work to stop the trafficking of MDMA throughout the United States. The list below is just a small sampling of operations reported on the DEA Web site:

The State Palace Theater Investigation. Starting in 1998, the New Orleans Division of the DEA worked with the United States Attorney's Office in New Orleans to address the problem of club drugs, including Ecstasy. This operation found that between four and five hundred teenagers and young adults had been treated at local emergency rooms for club drug overdoses following participation in rave events conducted at New Orleans's State Palace Theater. The corporation that owned the theater was fined one hundred thousand dollars.

Operation Bad Vibe. Initiated by the DEA Little Rock Resident Office in 1999, this operation targeted Cybertribe, a rave party promotion group responsible for distributing thousands of MDMA pills and other drugs in Arkansas. The organization was linked to traffickers in Tennessee and Florida. Law enforcement officials arrested more than fifty people and seized large quantities of MDMA, ketamine, and other club drugs.

Operation Green Clover. After a yearlong investigation that ended in August 2001, the DEA arrested dozens of traffickers and confiscated about eighty-five thousand tablets of Ecstasy and more than a million dollars in illegal drug money.

Operation Rave I and Rave II. In 2001 the DEA arrested 247 individuals and confiscated seven million tablets of Ecstasy, two million dollars in currency and more than one million in other assets. In this operation the DEA worked with the Israeli National Police, the German National Police, and numerous European partners.

Operation Candy Box. In March of 2004 the DEA arrested over 130 individuals in an American-Canadian crackdown on an Ecstasy and marijuana drug ring. The ring manufactured large quantities of Ecstasy and marijuana in Canada and then shipped them to cities around the United States. In addition to the large number of arrests, this three-year investigation resulted in the discovery that Ecstasy trafficking, which had largely been controlled by Russian and Israeli gangs, had now spread to groups with ties to Southeast Asia. The operation also disrupted a sizable money laundering business. DEA and FBI agents in New York City initiated operation

Candy Box in May 2001. It eventually became an operation encompassing sixteen cities in the U.S. and three in Canada. Large quantities of drugs and several manufacturing labs were also seized.

Despite these successes, U.S. authorities say Ecstasy continues to flood into the United States. U.S. Customs seized approximately 400,000 MDMA tablets in fiscal year 1997 compared with approximately 7.2 million tablets in 2001. On July 22, 2000 approximately 2.1 million tablets were seized in Los Angeles. To date, this is the largest seizure of MDMA tablets in the United States. Furthermore, DEA officials now report more and more violence connected with MDMA. In 2000 and 2001 MDMA distributors were involved in the murders of several other MDMA distributors and in shoot-outs with police officers in New York City and Detroit. DEA officials report that weapons are now routinely seized along with MDMA at the street level.

During the last two decades the number of prisoners in state and federal institutions has grown from 200,000 to more than a million. A striking example of the success—or perhaps the failure—of the American "War on Drugs" is that more than 30 percent of the current state prison population and 60 percent of prisoners in federal custody are serving time for drug offenses, including those involving MDMA use, possession, manufacture, and distribution. And yet, people continue using MDMA. Why do young people continue to use the drug when doing so poses health and legal risks? Kicking any substance abuse habit is far from easy— but not impossible.

ONE OF THE FIRST STEPS TOWARD BREAKING FREE OF A SUBSTANCE ABUSE HABIT
IS TO TALK WITH A COUNSELOR.

5 DESIGNING A DRUG-FREE LIFE

THE SIMPLE TRUTH is that Ecstasy is not safe to take even once, and certainly not on a regular basis. Taking MDMA may cause immediate changes in the brain and body that can lead to illness and even death. Recent research shows that the use of MDMA may lead to permanent brain damage, leading to memory loss and mood disorders, among other complications.

Possessing, using, manufacturing, or selling MDMA—or even the chemicals used to create it—is illegal. Possession of a single tablet can lead to jail time. Even if a prison term isn't mandatory, the stigma of having a felony conviction has life-long consequences.

Yet in spite of all this, nearly 9 percent of all teens students in the United States have tried Ecstasy at one time or another. Why do young people insist on risking their health and freedom to take illegal drugs like Ecstasy?

Research indicates that Ecstasy is not physically addictive. Most people do not experience physical symptoms of withdrawal—nausea, vomiting, fever, and even hallucinations—typically seen with drugs like cocaine, heroin, and alcohol. They also do not experience tolerance to the drug, in that they rarely need to take more and more of the drug to feel the same effects they once received at smaller doses.

However, many users describe becoming psychologically dependent on Ecstasy; that is, they don't feel "normal" without experiencing the drug's effects on their mood and behavior. MDMA acts in the brain as an antidepressant and antianxiety drug. If someone is under emotional strain or feeling depressed, MDMA can provide release and comfort. It is also true that many people take illicit drugs, including MDMA, when they suffer from a serious but undiagnosed underlying mental illness, such as clinical depression or anxiety.

Breaking Free

If an individual fears that he or she or a friend may be psychologically dependent on Ecstasy, or any other drug, the first step is to talk with a doctor or counselor. A doctor can help diagnose any underlying condition that may exist and be contributing to drug use. They can prescribe safe and legal medication to treat the condition.

Health professionals can help one to understand why he or she takes Ecstasy and can help devise a safe and effective plan to stop taking the drug. Such a plan can include taking part in one-on-one psychotherapy. Talking with a therapist can help to focus on the underlying reasons why Ecstasy is being used on a regular basis. A therapist can also develop a treatment plan to break an Ecstasy habit and replace drug use with other, more positive behaviors.

Stella, now a twenty-two-year-old college graduate, used Ecstasy on a regular—and heavy—basis during high school.

I only felt "normal" when I was high. I thought I could only be myself on X. It took me seeing a doctor and understanding how much of a risk I was taking with my health, to say nothing of what my behavior was doing to my family, to quit.

What Stella discovered, however, was that quitting Ecstasy was harder than it looked.

I thought I could just go cold turkey, so to speak. But I felt awful all the time—tired, anxious. My doctor helped me by prescribing some antidepressants that I took at night. They helped me to sleep and kind of got my body and brain back into balance. And then my doctor suggested that I go to meetings of a teen Narcotics Anonymous group, just to get another perspective and have a chance to talk about what I was going through. It was embarrassing at first, but after awhile, I really felt relieved. I wasn't alone, and there was no shame in what happened to me.

It took Stella about six months for all of the physical side effects to pass, and she still struggles with the emotional aftermath.

Breaking Bad Habits

The first step toward kicking a substance abuse habit is to admit that there is a problem. Recovery from abuse is a difficult process, and the user has to want to change. Parents, friends, a school counselor, or family doctor can offer help and support. Here are some thoughts on how to leave a bad habit behind:

Understand why. Perhaps, with the help of a therapist, the first step to breaking an Ecstasy habit is to look at how it began and why it continues. In other words, what is the payoff for continuing a negative behavior? For many users of Ecstasy (and other illicit drugs), the payoff is getting free of reality by letting the drug take over. For a short time the user feels better—free from problems and uninhibited.

Calculate the cost. But people with drug habits lose a great deal. For instance, someone dependent on an illegal substance may resort to stealing to pay for the habit, often lying to keep his or her behavior secret. Using Ecstasy, then, trades the temporary release of tension for long-term emotional health.

Choose to change. After weighing both sides of the issue—the payoff and tradeoff—it's time to make a choice. Using is no longer an involuntary act because a conscious choice is being made with each dose. Now comes the time to decide which is more valuable—the temporary (and dangerous) release provided by Ecstasy, or the strength and pride that comes from being independent, truthful, and confident.

Throw out the bad, bring in the good. A bad habit like Ecstasy abuse is usually started as a way to fill a need. There are as many excuses for taking Ecstasy as there are people who take it, which is why working with a therapist or physician to identify the underlying issues is important. However, no matter why one starts taking Ecstasy, new ways need to be found to fulfill the needs. An old habit will be replaced by a better, alternative action, going for a run when feeling stressed, for instance. Making good choices will lead to better self-esteem, which is key to kicking a substance abuse habit.

It is important to remember that substance abuse is treatable. The immediate goal of treatment is to reduce drug use, improve one's ability to function, and minimize the medical and social complications of drug abuse. The right program will teach the individual to take control and live a drug-free, productive life.

GLOSSARY

addiction: A pattern of behavior based on great physical and/or psychological need for a substance or activity. Addiction is characterized by compulsion, loss of control, and continued repetition of a behavior no matter what the consequences.

analogues: Drugs that are structurally similar to others but differ slightly in composition.

anesthetic: A substance that causes a loss of feeling and relieves pain.

antidepressant: Any of a number of drugs used to treat and relieve depression.

anxiety: Uneasiness, worry, uncertainly, and fear that come with thinking about an anticipated danger. Anxiety may be a normal reaction to a real threat or occur when no danger exists.

central nervous system (CNS): The nerve cells making up the brain and spinal cord.

depression: A mental disorder that involves not only feelings of sadness and despair but also slowed thinking, decreased pleasure, appetite changes, sleeping difficulties, and/or physical aches and pains.

designer drug: A synthetic drug produced by chemically altering the structure of an original drug, often in order to avoid laws against the original drug or to increase the appeal of the original drug.

dopamine: A neurotransmitter, or chemical messenger, in the brain.

hallucinogen: A substance that distorts the user's perception of the world around him/her or causes the user to perceive objects and events that are not real.

illicit: Illegal.

neurons: Nerve cells, the basic units of the nervous system. Neurons are able to conduct impulses and communicate by releasing and receiving chemical messengers called neurotransmitters.

neurotransmitters: Chemicals (including serotonin, dopamine, norepinephrine) that act to send nerve signals. Neurotransmitters are released by neurons. When an imbalance among the neurotransmitters occurs, emotional and physical symptoms result.

opiate: A drug derived from opium, designed to relieve pain.

serotonin: A neurotransmitter found in the brain and body that affects behavior, mood, memory, and appetite.

synapse: The gap between the nerve endings of two neurons. For a message to pass across the synapse, it needs help from a neurotransmitter.

tolerance: A condition in which a drug user needs increasing amounts of a drug to achieve the same level of intoxication once obtained from using smaller amounts.

withdrawal: A condition resulting from stopping the use of a drug. Symptoms may include intense physical and psychological cravings, fatigue, nausea, depression, and anxiety.

FURTHER INFORMATION

Books

Alvergue, Anne. *Ecstasy: The Danger of False Euphoria.* New York: Rosen Publishing Group, 1998.

Brenna, Kristine. *Ecstasy and Other Designer Drugs.* Philadelphia: Chelsea House Publishers, 2000.

Kuhn, Cynthia, Ph.D., Scott Scwartzwelder, Ph.D., and Wilkie Wilson, Ph.D. *Buzzed: The Straight Facts about the Most Abused Drugs from Alcohol to Ecstasy.* New York: W.W. Norton, 2003.

Kuhn, Cynthia, Scott Swartzwelder, and Wilkie Wilson. *Just Say Know: Talking with Kids about Drugs and Alcohol.* New York: W.W. Norton & Company, 2002.

Robbins, Paul. *Designer Drugs.* Springfield, NJ: Enslow Publishers, 1995.

Saunders, Nicholas. *E for Ecstasy.* London: Nicholas Saunders, 1993.

Medical Journals
Baggott, Matthew, et al. "Chemical analysis of Ecstasy pills." *Journal of the American Medical Association* 284 (2000): 2190.

Bankson, M. G. and K. A. Cunningham. "3, 4 Methylenedioxymethamphetamine (MDMA) as a unique model of serotonin receptor function and serotonin-dopamine interactions." *Journal of Pharmacology and Experimental Therapeutics* 297 (2001): 846-852.

Dafters, R. I. and E. Lynch. "Persistent loss of thermoregulation in the rate induced by 3, 4 methylenedioxymethamphetamine (MDMA or "Ecstasy") but not fenfluramine." *Psychopharmacology* 138 (1998): 207-212.

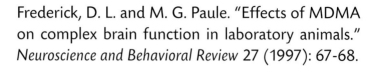

Frederick, D. L. and M. G. Paule. "Effects of MDMA on complex brain function in laboratory animals." *Neuroscience and Behavioral Review* 27 (1997): 67-68.

Johnson, L. D., O'Malley PM, and Bachman JG. *Monitoring the Future: National Survey Results on Drug Use, 1975-2000.* Bethesda, MD, 2000. (Updated annually).

Kish, S. J., et al. "Striatal serotonin is depleted in brain of human MDMA (Ecstasy) user." *Neurology* 55 (2000): 294-296.

Lester, S. J., et al. "Cardiovascular effects of 3, 4 methylenedioxymethamphetamine: A double-blind, placebo-controlled trial." *Annals of Internal Medicine* 133 (2000): 969-973.

Marston, H. M., et al. "Behavioral analysis of the acute and chronic effects of MDMA treatment in the rat." *Psychopharmacology* 144 (1999): 67-76.

Parrott, A. C. and J. Lasky. "Ecstasy (MDMA) effect upon mood and cognition: before, during, and after a Saturday night dance." *Psychopharmacology* 139 (1998): 261-268.

Web Sites

Information and Resources on Club Drugs
www.clubdrugs.org

National Drug Intelligence Center
www.usdoj.gov

National Institute on Drug Abuse
www.nida.nih.gov

Partnership for a Drug Free America
www.drugfreeamerica.org

INDEX

ABOUT THE AUTHOR

Suzanne LeVert is the author of more than twenty-five young adult and adult nonfiction titles. She specializes in health and medical subjects, as well as the social sciences. For Marshall Cavendish's Celebrate the States series, Ms. LeVert contributed *Massachusetts* and *Louisiana*. Born in Natick, Massachusetts, Ms. LeVert now practices law in New Orleans, Louisiana, where she comes face-to-face with the legal and social problems caused by illegal drug addiction and trafficking.